The Art of Making
Hand-Beaded
Bags

Karen Torrisi

Search Press

Acknowledgments

Thank you to my family for their endless encouragement, support and for instilling in me the belief that nothing is impossible to achieve, if you work hard enough.

Thank you also to my husband, Tim, for his eternal belief in my ability and his appreciation of my skill as a beader. Without his love and support none of this would have become a reality.

I would also like to thank the following people: Maisie Jarrett, for nurturing my love of beading and passing on her skills to me; Julie Stanton, at Kangaroo Press, for giving me the opportunity to write this book; my work colleagues, for the inspiration they give me and for their technical support.

First published in Great Britain in 2002 by
Search Press Ltd
Wellwood
North Farm Road
Tunbridge Wells
Kent TN2 3DR

Reprinted 2002, 2003

First published in Australia in 2002 by Kangaroo Press
An imprint of Simon & Schuster (Australia) Pty Limited
20 Barcoo Street, East Roseville NSW 2069

A Viacom Company
Sydney New York London

ISBN 1 903975 44 1

Cover and internal design by Anna Soo Design
Illustrations by Christian Collis
Typeset in 11/14pt Sabon
Printed in China by Everbest Printing Co.

Contents

Introduction

Beading has been a fashionable art form for thousands of years. It has been used to embellish clothing as far back as Egyptian times and is enjoying another strong revival in the new millennium.

Beaded handbags have always been treasured accessories. As far back as the second half of the nineteenth century, handbags were desired for their beauty as well as the exceptional workmanship used in their creation.

Modern beaded handbags take on many forms. Inspired by the treasures of the past, the bags of today vary in shape, style, colour and beaded techniques. We also have a much wider variety of beads to choose from than our predecessors with which to create a dazzling array of effects.

Beaded bags from the middle of the nineteenth century were almost always made with small fine beads. In the 1920s beads were lined with real 9 carat gold, before imitation metallic finishes were invented. Fringing and tassels were also commonly used in this era as an added point of decoration on handbags.

Today all types of beads are used, from sequins to crystal beads and stones, from bugle beads to pearls. It is the fusion of the many styles and mediums that makes the handbags of today just as sought after and collectable as their earlier counterparts.

My aim with this book is to introduce you to some of the techniques of beading.

The patterns I have created are to be a starting point and will help you with your first projects. Some are very simple, using only one beading technique while others combine various beading methods. I have created patterns using different shaped bags to give you a large selection of shapes and sizes.

All the projects are aimed at beginners through to more experienced beaders. I believe that with the clear explanation of each technique, your knowledge of beading will grow and you will learn much from the different directions and helpful hints.

I hope that your enthusiasm for learning hand beading will encourage you to complete a number of the beaded handbags in this book. I hope too that these treasured future heirlooms become extra precious because they have been crafted by your own hands.

Enjoy!

Equipment and materials

All the bags in this book have been pre-beaded then stitched together. You can also purchase pre-made articles and bead them.

The equipment you will need to bead the bags in this book are:

1. Beading needles

2. Polycotton thread. Colour matching will be outlined in the instructions of each bag

3. Stiff tulle fabric. Preferably white.

4. 2B lead pencil

5. Dressmakers' chalk pencils in a variety of colours suitable to draw on dark, medium and light coloured fabrics

6. A bead tray – a flat tray covered with a piece of neutral coloured felt. The beads will stay still while you pick them up. It is also easier to move your work if necessary. The lid from an ice cream container can also be used.

7. Small scissors

8. Iron – to press your work and fuse on interfacing

9. Small nosed pliers – to use in making beaded straps. Tigers tail, metal crimps, metal chain

10. 1 metric teaspoon – to measure beads

11. 1 ring frame (optional) approximately 26.5 cm (10 in) diameter

12. 100 cm (40 in) calico (optional) – for bias strips to wrap around the inner ring frame

Transferring a design

Choose your design.

Photocopy or trace your chosen design.

Leave about 2 cm (⅝ in) excess paper around the outer edge of the pattern (this will help when you pin the tulle to the design).

Take the white tulle and place it over the design.

Pin in place. Secure around all edges.

Using the 2B lead pencil, trace the design onto the tulle.

Trace the stitching line, the outer line of the pattern and the grain line of the pattern.

Select a sharpened chalk pencil.

Test the colour on a corner of the fabric, to make sure the markings are clear.

Make sure the fabric piece is slightly larger than the pattern to allow for any fraying.

Cut a piece of interfacing the same size as the fabric piece.

Using the iron, bond the glue side of the interfacing to the wrong side of the fabric. (Use hot dry heat and gentle even movements to avoid forming air bubbles or creases in the fabric.) Make sure the interfacing is properly fixed before you begin the project.

Pin the tulle pattern onto the fabric, making sure the pattern grain line is parallel with the selvedge of the fabric.

Using the pencil line as a guide, chalk the pattern onto the fabric.

If you are worried about losing any detailed part of the design, hand tack along any major lines after tracing the whole design.

To secure the layers together and create a stitching guide, hand or machine tack the stitching line around the bag. This will help keep the finished handbag shape even while the beading is worked.

Now you are ready to begin a project.

Techniques

Starting your work

Thread your needle. Tie a knot at the end of the thread whether it is single or double thread. Take your needle up through your fabric to the right side, unless specified otherwise. Always bring your needle up at the start of your line, in the centre of the line marking.

Finishing your work

Take your needle down, through to the wrong side of the fabric. Make sure there is at least 7 cm (2¾ in) of thread length in your needle, if you have less than this you will find it difficult to continue with the following step. Sew 2 small stitches in a whip stitch motion at the back of your work. Cut your thread leaving approximately 1 cm (⅜ in) remaining at the back of your work.

Running stitch

Cup Sequin
1. Cut a piece of thread approximately 40 cm (16 in) in length.
2. Thread the needle with a single thread.
3. Tie a knot at one end of the thread.

> Note: Always work towards you, turning your work if necessary.
> Roll excess fabric in at edges, do not scrunch up fabric.

4. Bring the needle through to the right side of the fabric. With the needle, pick up the sequin dome side first. The curved side of the sequin will be facing up. (If you pick up the sequin curved side first, the dome side of the sequin will be facing up.) Let the sequin slide down the thread and sit on the fabric.
5. Holding the sequin in place, take your needle down the right side of the sequin through to the wrong side of the fabric.
6. Bring the needle back up through the fabric to the left side ahead of the sequin, but right next to its edge.
7. Take the needle back down through the fabric to the wrong side through the centre hole in the sequin.
8. Bring the needle back up through the fabric to the left side, approximately half the size of the sequin away from the last sequin that you stitched in place.
9. Repeat steps 4–8. See diagram on the following page.

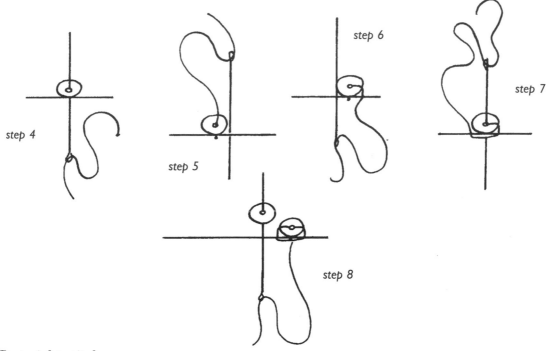

step 4

step 5

step 6

step 7

step 8

BB straight stitch

Bugle beads

1. Cut a piece of thread approximately 80 cm (32 in) in length.
2. Thread the needle with a single thread.
3. Bring both strands of thread together at the ends and tie them in a knot, to form a double thread.
4. Bring your needle up through to the right side of the fabric.
5. Thread 1 bugle bead onto your needle, let it slip down your thread.
6. Lay the bugle bead down along the marked line (this is an easy way to anticipate its length).
7. Take the needle down, through to the wrong side of the fabric at this point. Pull the thread firmly.
8. Bring the needle back up through the fabric to the right side, a few millimetres away from the point at which you took the thread down, along the marked line. Pull the thread firm.
9. Repeat steps 4–8. See diagram below with each bugle bead until you reach the end of the line. Finish off, see Finishing your work.

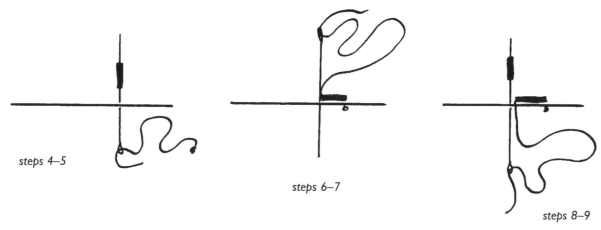

steps 4–5

steps 6–7

steps 8–9

Straight stitch

Seed beads

1. Cut a piece of thread approximately 80 cm (32 in) in length.
2. Thread the needle with a single thread.
3. Bring both strands of thread together at the ends and tie them in a knot to form a double thread.
4. Bring the needle up, through to the right side of the fabric.
5. Thread 1 seed bead onto the needle, let it slide down the thread.
6. Consider the size of the bead. This will form the length of the stitch.
7. Using the needle, pick up a few threads of fabric along the marked line, on the right side of the fabric, and slide the needle along.
8. Repeat steps 5–7 until each line of stitching is complete. See diagram.

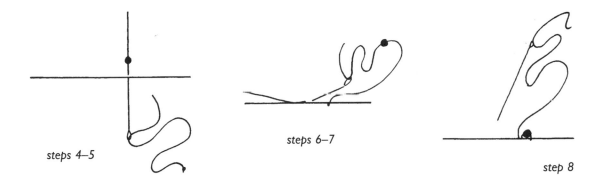

steps 4–5   *steps 6–7*   *step 8*

Single seed bead

1. Cut a piece of thread approximately 80 cm (32 in) long.
2. Thread the needle with a single thread.
3. Bring both strands of thread together at the ends and tie them in a knot to form a double thread.
4. Bring the needle up, through to the right side of the fabric on one side of the marked point.
5. With the needle pick up one seed bead.
6. Take the needle down, through to the wrong side of the fabric, just next to the seed bead. See diagram below.

> Note: The length of your stitch should be the same size as your bead

7. Repeat this step as often as marked. This method is also suitable for fill in work, just keep the angles of your beads random and close.

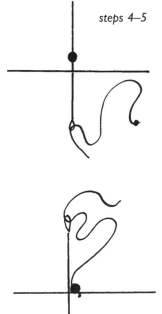

steps 4–5

step 6

5

Seed bead anchor (centre hole)

1. Cut a piece of thread 80 cm (32 in) in length.
2. Thread the needle with a single thread.
3. Bring both strands together at the ends and tie them in a knot to form a double thread.
4. Bring the needle up to the right side of the fabric where you would anticipate the centre of the bead to be, or where there is a mark for the bead placement.
5. Pick up either 1 sequin or 1 crystal rosette with your needle.
6. Let your sequin/crystal drop down your thread and rest on the fabric.
7. Using the needle, pick up 1 seed bead.
8. Take the needle back down through the hole in your sequin/crystal to the wrong side of the fabric. Pull firmly. Your seed bead should sit on top of your sequin/crystal, forming an anchor point. See diagram below.
9. Finish off on the wrong side of the fabric.

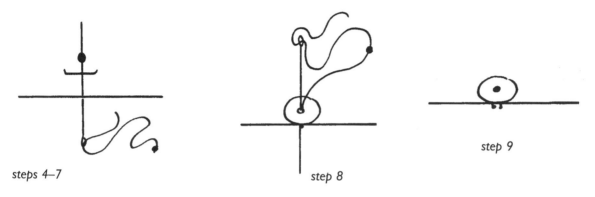

steps 4–7   step 8   step 9

Bricking

1. This technique is used when sewing bugle beads side by side to fill in a designated space.
2. Using a BB straight stitch, begin by beading the outer edges of your design.
3. If working on a ray pattern, i.e. as for the Radiating Antique Style handbag design, begin at the centre of the design and work outwards.
4. When beading your second row of bugle beads, keep them close to the first row and aim to stitch this centre bugle bead over the space between the 2 bugle beads below.
5. Continue stitching this second row of bugle beads.
6. Repeat for all subsequent rows.
7. For any small obvious spaces sew in a size 1 bugle bead.

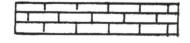

Sew on rhinestones

1. Use a marked cross as a guide for placement.
2. Thread the needle with a single thread.
3. Bring both strands of thread together and tie in a knot, to form a double thread.
4. Bring the threaded needle up, through to the right side of the fabric, on one corner of the marked cross.
5. Thread the rhinestone onto your needle.
6. Take the needle down, through to the wrong side of the fabric, on the diagonally opposite side of the cross. Your stitch should be the same size as the rhinestone and be firm.
7. Bring the needle back up, to the right side of the fabric, on the other side of the cross.
8. Thread the needle through the channel on the back of the rhinestone.
9. Take the needle down through the fabric to the wrong side at the point where the needle came out of the channel of the rhinestone. See diagram below.
10. Finish off.

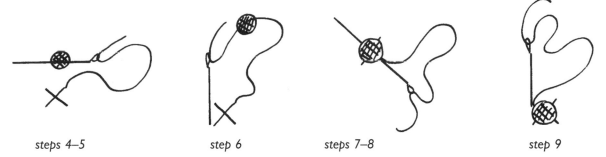

steps 4–5   step 6   steps 7–8   step 9

Sequin flower

1. Cut a piece of thread approximately 80 cm (32 in) in length.
2. Thread the needle with a single thread.
3. Bring both strands together at the ends and tie them in a knot, to form a double thread.
4. Stitch the centre rhinestone using the Sew on Rhinestone technique.
5. Use 5 marked lines around the rhinestone as a guide to the placement of the sequin petals. See diagram.
6. Bring the needle up, to the right side of the fabric, next to the rhinestone on one side of the 5 marked lines.
7. Using the needle, thread 2 seed beads and 1 sequin (right side up) onto the thread.
8. Leaving a 2 mm space from the initial stitch and using the marked guideline, take the needle down through to the wrong side of the fabric. See diagram.
9. Repeat steps 6–8 for all 5 prongs of the flower.
10. Finish off.

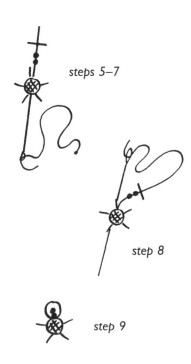

steps 5–7

step 8

step 9

Beaded loop

1. Cut a piece of thread approximately 80 cm (32 in) in length.
2. Thread the needle with a single thread.
3. Bring both strands of thread together at the ends and tie a knot to form a double thread.
4. The placement dots represent the centres of the loops.
5. Bring the needle up, through to the right side of the fabric at the marked dot.
6. Using your needle, pick up 1 sequin (right side up).
7. Thread on 9 seed beads, then 1 pearl then 8 seed beads.
8. Take your needle down through the first seed bead and the sequin, to the wrong side of the fabric.
9. Pull firmly but not too tightly, as the loops should hang and not stand away from your fabric.
10. Repeat this step along each marked line. See diagram.

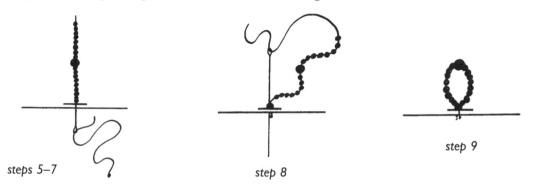

steps 5–7   step 8   step 9

Triple seed loop encrusting

1. Cut a piece of thread approximately 80 cm (32 in) in length.
2. Thread the needle with a single thread.
3. Bring both strands together at the end and tie them in a knot to form a double thread.
4. Make sure the pre-marked design is outlined in seed or bugle beads first using their respective methods.
5. Start work close to the edge. Bring the needle up, through to the right side of the fabric.
6. Using the needle, thread 3 seed beads onto the thread.
7. Take the needle down, through to the wrong side of the fabric at a point approximately 1 bead width away from where you brought up the needle up in Step 5. See diagram.
8. Repeat Steps 5–7 close together and all in random directions until the space is filled.
9. Your work should be slightly raised.

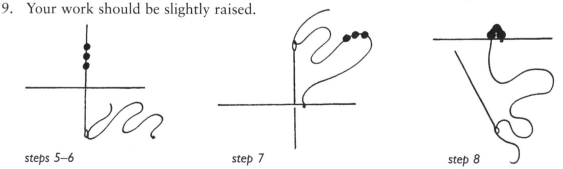

steps 5–6   step 7   step 8

Loose loop fringing

1. Cut a piece of thread approximately 200 cm (79 in) in length.
2. Thread the needle with a single thread.
3. Bring both strands of thread together at the ends and tie them in a knot, to form a double thread.
4. Bring the needle up, through to the right side of the fabric, at the edge of the handbag.
5. Thread on the desired number of beads. Remember the amount be halved once the loop is formed. For loose loop and fringed handbags thread on enough beads to measure 50 cm (20 in) to form 25 cm (10 in) loops.
6. Take the needle down, through to the wrong side of the fabric, a bead width away from the previous point.
7. Bring your needle back through to the right side of the fabric 1 bead width away from your last point.
8. Repeat Steps 5–6 as many times as the length of thread allows.
9. You will start and finish off, on average, every 2 fringed loops.

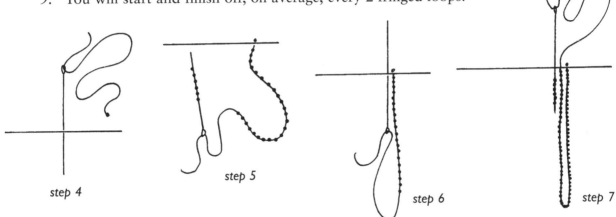

step 4 *step 5* *step 6* *step 7*

Loop border

1. Cut a piece of thread approximately 80 cm (32 in) in length.
2. Thread the needle with a single thread.
3. Bring both strands of thread together at the ends and tie them in a knot to form a double thread.
4. Bring the needle up through to the right side of the fabric, at the beginning of the top line. See diagram.
5. Thread 8 beads onto your needle.
6. Take the needle back down, through to the wrong side of the fabric on the lower line, directly beneath the point at the top line where you began.
7. Bring your needle up 1 bead width away on the lower line.
8. Repeat Step 5.
9. Take the needle down, through to the wrong side of the fabric, on the top line directly above the last point on the lower line.
10. Repeat Steps 4–10 until the line is finished.

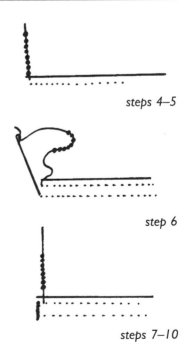

steps 4–5

step 6

steps 7–10

Loop ended fringing

1. Cut a piece of thread approximately 160 cm (63 in) in length.
2. Thread the needle with a single thread.
3. Bring both strands of thread together at the ends and tie them in a knot, to form a double thread.
4. Bring the needle up, through to the right side of the fabric, at the first loop marking.
5. Thread on the desired number of beads.
6. Thread on a large feature bead.
7. Thread on the beads that will form the loop.
8. Thread the needle back through the large feature bead, then thread on the same number of beads as in Step 5.
9. Take the needle back through the fabric to the wrong side approximately 1 bead width away from the point at which you came up in Step 4.
10. Continue beading at each point that is marked using Steps 4–9.

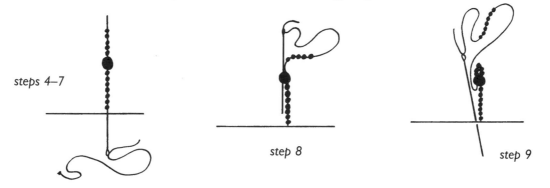

steps 4–7

step 8

step 9

Beading on a ring frame for fill in work – setting up

1. Ensure the design is traced onto a square of fabric. Do not cut around the bag shape.
2. Choose a ring frame large enough to accommodate the size of the whole bag in the centre of the frame, 26 ½ cm (10 ½ in) diameter. Bead the necessary features of the bag first (anything other than the fill in work).
3. Cut calico bias strips. Wrap them around the inner ring of the frame, pulling tightly so the binding grips to itself. Cover the whole inner ring and glue the end of the calico on the inside of the ring. Pin in place until glue is dry.
4. Place your fabric with the design in the centre, over the inner ring.
5. Place the outer ring over the fabric and down onto the inner ring.
6. Pull the fabric evenly until it is as tight as a drum. Tighten the screw on the outer ring as you go, to hold the fabric in place.
7. When satisfied with the tautness of the fabric, fully tighten the screw. Now you are ready to bead the fill in work.

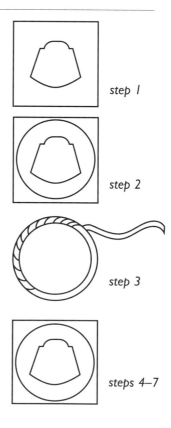

step 1

step 2

step 3

steps 4–7

Projects

Flat sequin covered handbag

You will need

40 cm (16 in) delustered satin fabric
40 cm (16 in) lining fabric
40 cm (16 in) woven fusible interfacing, medium weight
1 spool light silver metallic thread No. 40
1 large press stud
81 cm (32 in) of thick twisted cord
1 spool 120 thick polycotton, colour to match fabric
3 teaspoons 6 mm cup sequins, metallic finish
3 teaspoons 6 mm cup sequins, clear and iridescent finish

Method

Transfer the markings for the beading. Refer to Transferring a Design on page 2.

Start with the large outer curved lines. The cup sequins in this section of the design are to have the curved side of the sequin facing up.

Stitch using the Running Stitch Cup Sequin technique on page 3.

Brick your sequins, see diagram below. Do the best you can with the curved lines. The smaller the curve becomes the less beads you will fit in the line. Leave a little extra space in between sequins if this helps.

For this style I have used a metallic sequin and a transparent sequin. These are used to achieve a subtle contrast within the shade of the colour. You can use any colour combination for this style.

Next, bead all the horizontal lines, starting at the top straight edge.

'Brick' your sequins. The sequins should slot into each other perfectly.

Stitch using the Running Stitch technique on page 3, the dome side of the cup sequins are to be facing up.

Make a conscious effort to keep the lines straight and even. If necessary, slot in the final sequin in each row so that it sits under the sequin in the curved line. Gaps will make the work look uneven and messy.

After fully beading, give the work a gentle dry press face down underneath a towel. This will smooth out any uneven tension.

You are now ready to sew the bag together. Refer to Stitching Instructions for Flat Base Handbags and corded strap on page 50.

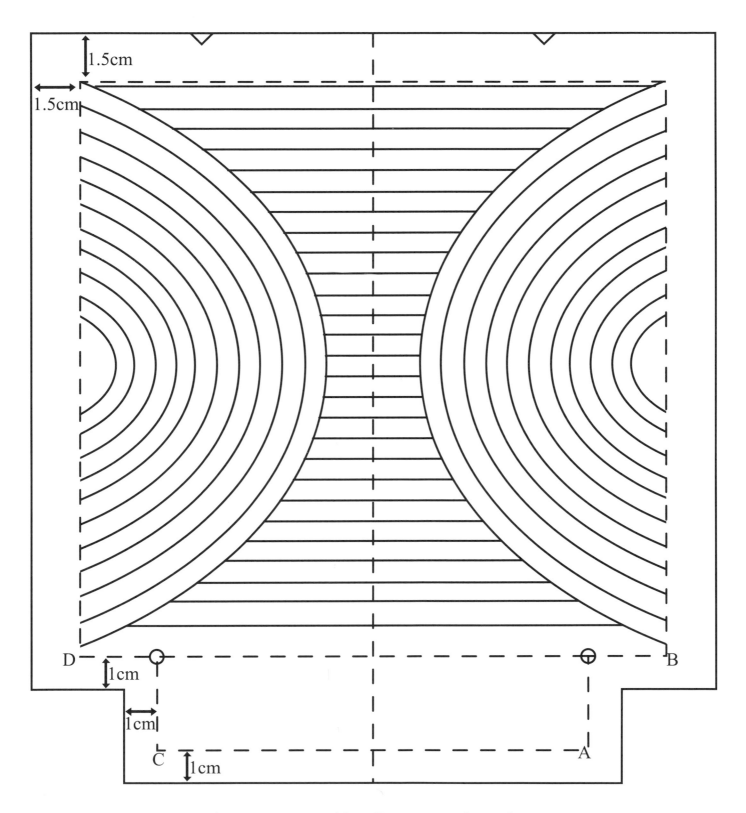

Flat sequin covered handbag (90% of actual size)

Sprinkle seed flower handbag

You will need

26 cm (10¼ in) Thai silk fabric
26 cm (10¼ in) woven fusible interfacing medium weight
26 cm (10¼ in) lining
48 cm (19 in) tiger tail
2 crimps
1 spool 120 thick polycotton, colour to match beads
3 teaspoons seed beads, size 10 (strap and bag)
1 teaspoon seed beads, size 8 (bag only)
67 pcs x 4 mm 5301 diamond shaped crystals (strap and bag)
½ teaspoon seed beads, size 11 (for strap only)
15 pcs x 6 mm tiger's eye beads (strap only)
5 pcs x 8 mm hand painted glass beads (strap only)
5 pcs x 7 mm hand painted ceramic beads (strap only)

Method

Double bond the fabric with interfacing, by fusing 2 layers of interfacing one at a time.

This will make the fabric extra stiff.

Transfer the markings for the beading. Refer to Transferring a Design, on page 2.

For this style you must stitch the top edge of the bag together before beading. Refer to Stitching Instructions for Top Edge of a Flat Base Handbag.

You are now ready to bead your bag.

Bead all clusters one at a time. Refer to Single Seed Bead technique on page 5. For the 4 seed flowers, start from the centre and bead in an outward direction with each seed. Keep the seeds close, as in a cross configuration, using the Single Seed Bead technique.

After stitching on all the beads, the bag is ready to be sewn together. Refer to Stitching Instructions for a Flat Base Handbag on page 50.

Make the beaded strap. Refer to Beaded Strap Instructions on page 59.

Bead configuration for the strap

Step 1	1 x 5301 + 1 x seed sz 10 + 1 x seed sz 11 + 1 x 5301 + 1 x seed sz 11 + 1 x seed sz 10.
Step 2	1 x 6 mm + 1 x seed sz 10 + 1 x seed sz 11 + 1 x 5301 + 1 x seed sz 11 + 1 x seed sz 10.
Step 3	Repeat Step 2, three times in total.
Step 4	1 x 8 mm +
Step 5	1 x seed sz 10 + 1 x seed sz 11 + 1 x 5301 + 1 x seed sz 11 + 1 seed sz 10.

Step 6   1 x 6 mm + 1 x step 5 + 1 x 7 mm + 1 x step 5 + 1 x 6 mm + 1 x step 5 + 1 x 8 mm + 1 x step 5 + 1 x 6 mm + 1 x step 5 + 1 x 7 mm + 1 x step 5 + 1 x 6 mm + 1 x step 5 + 1 x 8 mm + 1 x step 5 + 1 x 6 mm + 1 x step 5 + 1 x 7 mm + 1 x step 5 + 1 x 6 mm + 1 x step 5 + 1 x 8 mm + 1 x step 5 + 1 x 6 mm + 1 x step 5 + 1 x 7 mm + 1 x step 5 + 1 x 6 mm + 1 x step 5 + 1 x 8 mm + 1 x step 5 + 1 x 6 mm + 1 x step 5 + 1 x 7 mm + 1 x step 5.

Step 7   Repeat Step 2, twice.

Step 8   1 x 6 mm +

Step 9   Step 1.

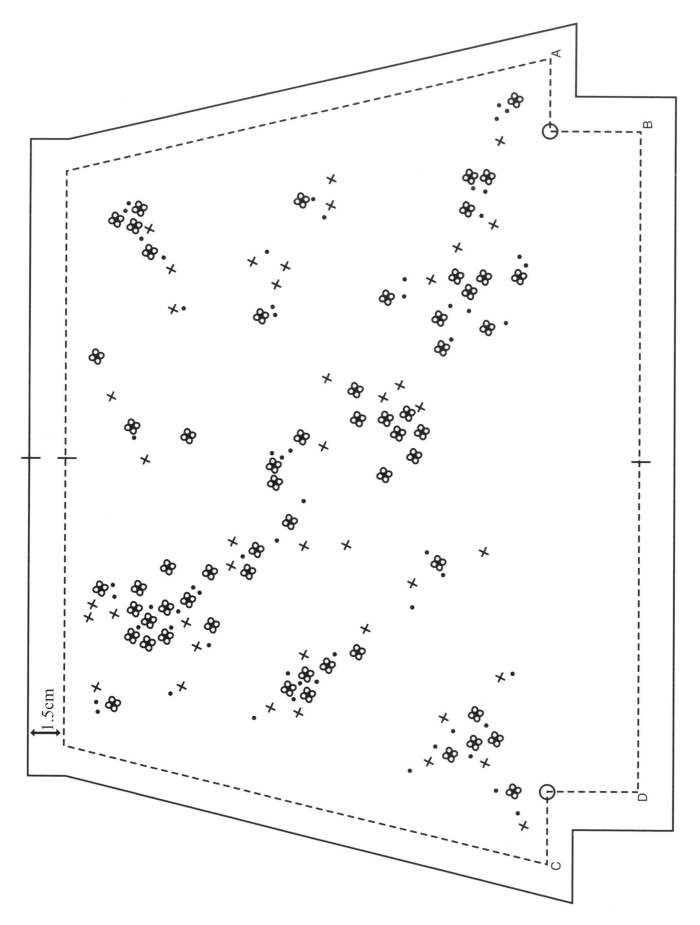

Sprinkle seed flower handbag (60% of actual size)

1.5cm

A

B

C

D

a sequin covered handbag

Left: Sequin rays and rosette handbag
Right: Geometric antique handbag

Left: Radiating antique style handbag
Right: Loose loop and fringed handbag

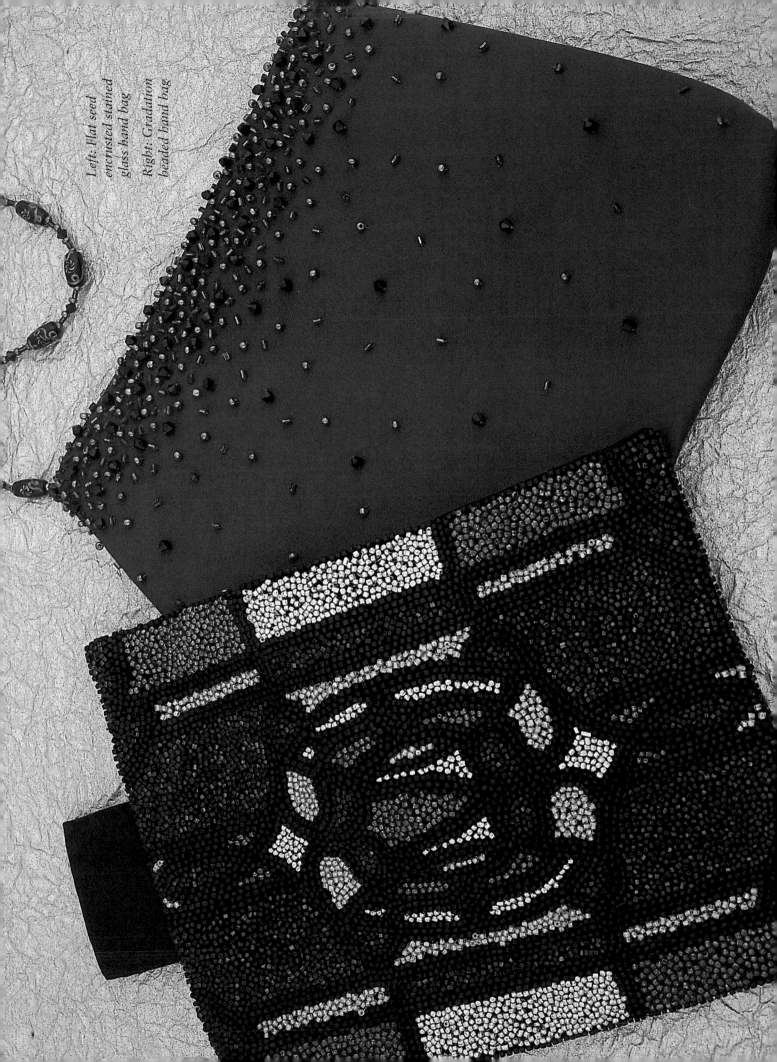

Left: Flat seed
encrusted stained
glass hand bag

Right: Gradation
beaded hand bag

Chinese brocade shoulder bag with hanging beading

You will need

45 cm (18 in) Chinese silk brocade fabric
45 cm (18 in) woven fusible interfacing medium weight
45 cm (18 in) lining
1 spool 120 thick polycotton, colour to match beads
250 cm (100 in) tiger tail
8 crimps
5 pcs x 8 mm hand painted glass beads
20 pcs x 6 mm round cut glass crystals
20 pcs x 7 mm round cut glass crystals
53 pcs x 4 mm pressed crystals
7 teaspoons seed beads, size 10 (red)
3 teaspoons seed beads, size 10 (pink)
3 teaspoons seed beads, size 11 (light green)
3 teaspoons seed beads, size 11 (dark green)
5 teaspoons 2 cut beads (red)

Method

Stitch the bag together first. Refer to Stitching Instructions for Shoulder Bags on page 52.

Transfer the markings for the beading. Refer to Transferring a Design on page 2.

For the border, refer to Loop Border technique on page 9.

Bead all of border first.

Next, bead the hanging loops at the front of the bag.

Thread a 150 cm (60 in) piece of thread.

Start all hanging loops from the right-hand side of the bag as you are looking at it.

Bring the needle up to the right side of the fabric at the furthest point on the right.

Notice this point has a symbol.

Thread the beads onto the needle and let them drop down onto the thread.

Once all the beads for that loop have been threaded, take the needle back down through the fabric to the wrong side, at the matching symbol on the left hand side of the bag. Repeat these steps for all hanging beading loops.

Bead configuration for hanging loops.

'x' mark
Thread on: 62 seed + 1 x 4 mm + 6 seed + 1 x 4 mm + 13 seed + 1 x 4 mm + 29 seed + 1 x 4 mm + 13 seed + 1 x 4 mm + 2 seed + 1 x 6 mm + 25 seed + 1 x 4 mm + 21 seed + 1 x 4 mm + 35 seed + 1 x 4 mm + 23 seed + 1 x 4 mm + 27 seed.

'o' mark

Thread on: 10 seed + 1 x 4 mm + 32 seed + 1 x 4 mm + 5 seed + 1 x 4 mm + 20 seed + 1 x 8 mm + 21 seed + 1 x 4 mm + 10 seed + 1 x 4 mm + 27 seed + 1 x 4 mm + 29 seed + 1 x 4 mm + 8 seed + 1 x 4 mm + 14 seed.

'A' mark

Thread on: 25 seed + 1 x 4 mm + 16 seed + 1 x 4 mm + 10 seed + 1 x 4 mm + 26 seed + 1 x 7 mm + 22 seed + 1 x 4 mm + 13 seed + 1 x 4 mm + 23 seed.

'B' mark

Thread on: 15 seed + 1 x 4 mm + 32 seed + 1 x 4 mm + 10 seed + 1 x 4 mm + 4 seed + 1 x 4 mm + 26 seed + 1 x 4 mm + 22 seed + 1 x 6 mm + 1 seed + 1 x 4 mm + 9 seed + 1 x 4 mm + 34 seed + 1 x 4 mm + 17 seed + 1 x 4 mm +23 seed.

'C' mark

Thread on: 36 seed + 1 x 4 mm + 27 seed + 1 x 4 mm + 6 seed + 1 x 4 mm + 15 seed + 1 x 4 mm + 12 seed + 1 x 7 mm + 1 x 4 mm + 21 seed + 1 x 4 mm + 33 seed + 1 x 4 mm + 19 seed.

'D' mark

Thread on: 11 seed + 1 x 4 mm + 7 seed + 1 x 4 mm + 43 seed + 1 x 4 mm + 33 seed + 1 x 8 mm + 30 seed + 1 x 4 mm + 4 seed + 1 x 4 mm + 30 seed + 1 x 4 mm + 27 seed.

'E' mark

Thread on: 46 seed + 1 x 4 mm + 34 seed + 1 x 4 mm + 13 seed + 1 x 4 mm + 2 seed + 1 x 8 mm + 19 seed + 1 x 4 mm + 19 seed + 1 x 4 mm + 33 seed + 1 x 4 mm + 12 seed + 1 x 4 mm + 27 seed.

Hanging loops on lower edge corners

Loop 1: Thread on 29 seed + 1 x 8 mm + 7 seed + thread the thread back through the 8 mm + 29 seed. Finish off.

Loop 2: Thread on 23 seed + 1 x 7 mm + 7 seed + thread the thread back through the 7 mm + 23 seed. Finish off.

Loop 3: Thread on 18 seed + 1 x 6 mm + 5 seed + thread the thread back through the 6 mm and + 18 seed. Finish off.

Repeat the above steps for the other corner.

Beaded strap

Refer to Beaded Strap instructions on page 59, the only difference being you are working with 2 strands.

Thread on the seed beads on each strand.

Take both strands through the crystal.

Repeat these 2 steps over and over for the whole strap until it is complete.

Bead configuration

13 x 2 cut beads + 1 x 7 mm + 15 seed sz 10 (red) + 1 x 6 mm.

Repeat this step 8 times + 13 x 2 cut beads.

Repeat for other strap.

Stitch the straps onto the bag at the marks indicated, 1 cm below the top edge. Cover this point in beads to hide the crimps.

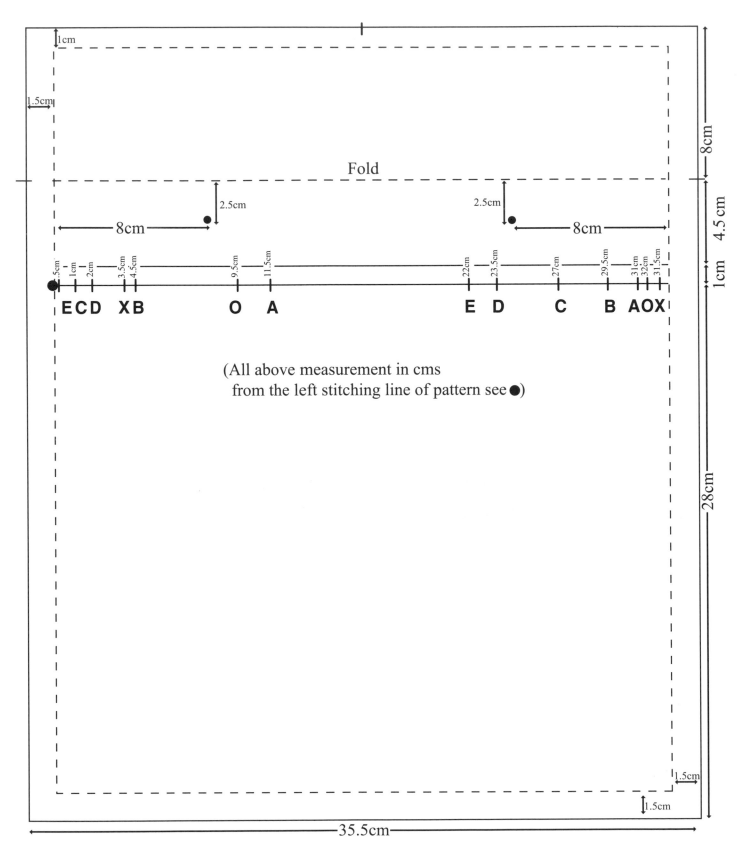

Fold

1cm

1.5cm

8cm

2.5cm

2.5cm

8cm

8cm

4.5 cm

1cm

.5cm
1cm
2cm
3.5cm
4.5cm
9.5cm
11.5cm
22cm
23.5cm
27cm
29.5cm
31cm
32cm
31.5cm

E C D X B   O A   E D   C   B AOX

(All above measurement in cms
from the left stitching line of pattern see ●)

28cm

1.5cm

1.5cm

35.5cm

Note: For lining cut two pieces 35.5 cm x 25 cm.

Chinese brocade bag with hanging beading (50% of actual size)

Chinese brocade shoulder bag with bead loops

You will need

45 cm (18 in) Chinese silk brocade fabric
45 cm (18 in) woven fusible interfacing medium weight
45 cm (18 in) lining
1 spool 120 thick polycotton, colour to match fabric
42 pcs x 4 mm 5301 diamond shaped crystals (green)
63 pcs x 5 mm 5301 diamond shaped crystals (yellow)
43 pcs x 4 mm 5301 diamond shaped crystals (amethyst)
73 pcs x 5 mm pressed crystals (amethyst)
41 pcs x 4 mm pearl (green)
4 teaspoons seed beads, size 8 (amethyst)
4 teaspoons 2 cut beads (green)
9 pcs x ornate beads or discs

Method

Stitch the bag together first. Refer to Stitching Instructions for Shoulder Bags on page 52.

Stitch straps onto the bag. Leave the lining open at the bottom edge to make it easier to start and finish off.

Transfer the markings for the beading. Refer to Transferring a Design on page 2. Centre the pattern on the finished bag and transfer the markings for the beading. Bead the design on the bag. Refer to Loop Border technique on page 9. The only difference being that you use the markings as a guide to where the beads will be placed.

Also thread on 2 seeds + 1 x crystal + 1 x 2 cut bead alternatively.

Next bead the straps.

Measure and make a mark every 2.5 cm (1 in). Stitch on the beads. Refer to Loop Border technique. Start and finish underneath the beads on the right side of the strap.

Finally, along the finished hem edge of the bag, make a mark every 1.3 cm (½ in).

These will be the points of reference for the beaded loops and crystals.

Stitch on the beaded loops. Refer to Loop Ended Fringing technique on page 10.

Loop configuration

Short loop: 1 x seed + 1 x 2 cut + 1 x seed + 1 x 5 mm pressed + 1 x seed + 1 x 2 cut + 1 x seed + 1 x 5 mm 5301 + 1 x seed + 1 x 2 cut + 1 x seed + 1 x 5 mm pressed + 1 x seed + 1 x 2 cut + 1 x seed.

Long loop: Thread on enough beads to measure 10 cm (4 in).

Hanging loop order

1. 1 long loop + 1 short loop +

2. 1x 5 mm 5301 + 1 short loop + 1 long loop + 1 short loop +
3. Repeat Step 2, 6 times.
4. 1 x 5 mm 5301 + 1 short loop + 1 long loop.

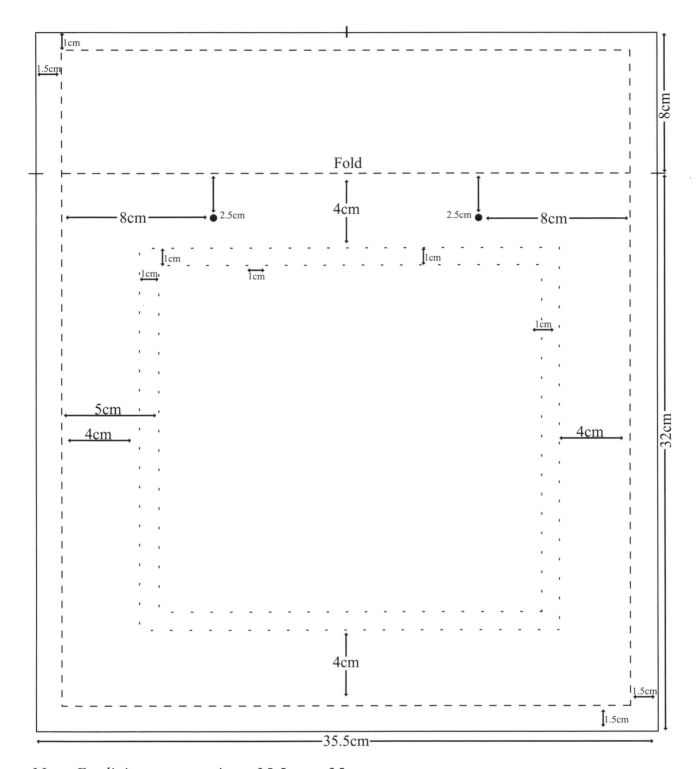

Note: For lining cut two pieces 35.5 cm × 25 cm.

Chinese brocade shoulder bag with bead loops (50% of actual size)

Beaded loop handbag

You will need

23 cm (9 in) Thai silk fabric
23 cm (9 in) woven fusible interfacing
23 cm (9 in) lining
1 spool 120 thick polycotton colour to match base fabric
90 pcs 4 mm pearl
15 teaspoons size 10 seed beads
2 teaspoons 5 mm square sequins (you can also substitute these with 6 mm flat round sequins with a centre hole, if square sequins are not available).

Method

Transfer the markings for the beading. Refer to Transferring a Design on page 2.

Begin with the loops on the second line from the bottom of the bag.

Work each line in an upward direction. Your loops will hang down and stay out of your way while you work.

Work from right to left (for left handers reverse this working direction).

Follow the Beaded Loop technique on page 8.

Bead all of the bag this way and on the flat.

When you have finished working these loops, stitch the bag together using the Stitching Instructions for Single Loop Handbags on page 55.

Once your bag is stitched together, bead the last row of beading at the bottom of the bag.

Instead of working your needle up and down straight through the fabric, slide it across from point to point.

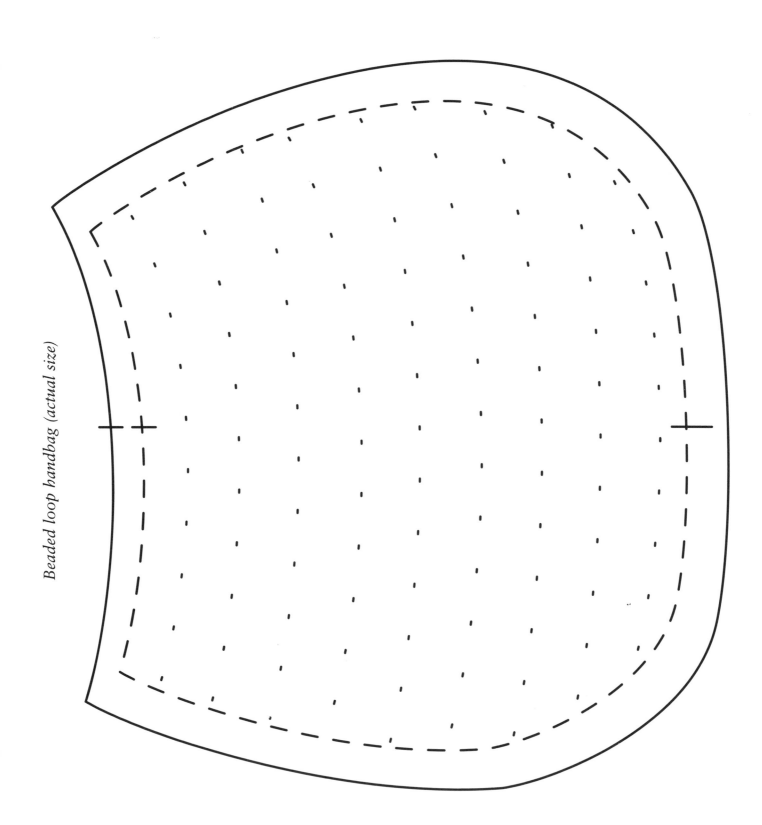

Beaded loop handbag (actual size)

Flat sequin flower and seed spray handbag

You will need

23 cm (9 in) Thai silk fabric
23 cm (9 in) woven fusible interfacing
23 cm (9 in) lining
1 large press stud
1 teaspoon 6 mm flat sequins
3 teaspoons 2 cut beads
8 pcs size 20 sew on rhinestones
1 spool of 120 thick polycotton, colour to match base fabric

Method

Bead your project before you stitch the bag together.

Transfer the markings for the beading. Refer to Transferring a Design on page 2.

Start with beading the sequin flowers. See Sequin Flower technique on page 7.

Finish off each flower separately.

Next bead the sprays using the Single Seed Bead technique on page 5.

Once you have finished the sprays, the bag is ready to be sewn together. Refer to Stitching Instructions for Single Loop Handbags on page 55.

Flat sequin flower and seed spray handbag (actual size)

Sequin rays and rosette handbag

You will need

40 cm (16 in) silk duchess satin
40 cm (16 in) woven fusible interfacing
40 cm (16 in) lining fabric
1 spool 120 thick polycotton, colour to match your base fabric
81 cm (32 in) thick twisted cord
1 large press stud
17 pcs 6 mm rosette crystals (holes in the centres)
2 teaspoons 6 mm flat sequins
3 teaspoons bugle beads, size 3
2 teaspoons seed beads, size 10

Method

Transfer the markings for the beading. Refer to Transferring a Design on page 2.

Bead each line one at a time, starting at the sequin end (the lower edge of the bag).

Work the beading before you sew the bag together.

Sew on the beads at the beginning of the first outer line, using the Seed Bead Anchor (centre hole) technique on page 6.

Repeat this method for each sequin, making sure that each sequin sits as close as possible to the previous one sewn.

The marked interval on the line is where you begin stitching on the bugle beads.

If your thread is too short by this stage, finish off and begin with a new thread.

Use BB Straight Stitch Bugle Bead technique on page 4.

Finish off at the end of each line after you have stitched your bugle beads down.

Each spray at the top of the lines is beaded separately.

Start with the rosette crystal. Use the Seed Bead Anchor (centre hole) technique to stitch the rosette down.

Continue on with the scatter of seed beads, using the Single Seed Bead technique on page 5. Finish off after each spray.

When finished, give your work a gentle dry press, faced down underneath a towel. This will smooth out any uneven tension. Be careful not to melt the sequins with too strong a heat from your iron.

You are now ready to sew the bag together.

Refer to Stitching Instructions for Flat Base Handbags and corded strap on page 50.

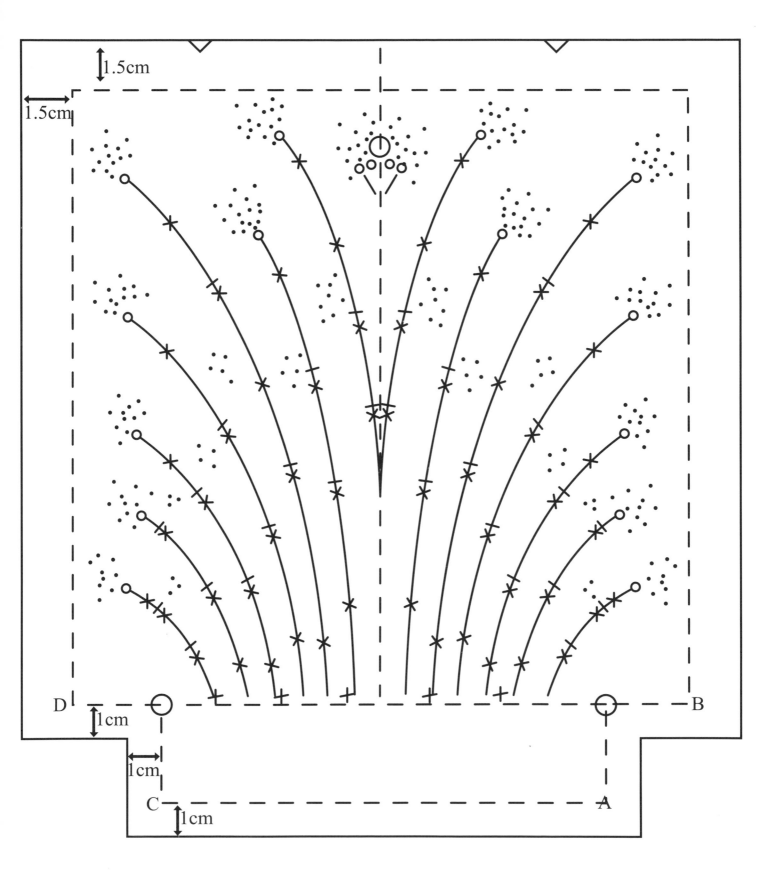

Sequin rays and rosette handbag (90% of actual size)

Gradation beaded handbag

You will need

26 cm (10 ¼ in) delustered satin fabric
26 cm (10 ¼ in) woven fusible interfacing
26 cm (10 ¼ in) lining
1 spool 120 thick polycotton, colour to match fabric
48 cm (19 in) tiger tail
2 crimps
90 pcs 4 mm 5301 diamond shaped crystals. (x marks on the pattern)
1 teaspoon bugle beads, size 1
20 pcs oval ornate ceramic hand painted beads (strap only)
2 teaspoons seed beads, size 8

Method

Double bond your fabric with interfacing, fusing 2 layers of interfacing one at a time. This will make your fabric extra stiff.

Transfer the markings for the beading. Refer to Transferring a Design on page 2.

For this style you must stitch the top edge of the bag together before beading. Refer to Stitching Instructions for Top Edge of Flat Base Handbags on page 57.

You are now ready to bead your bag.

x markings on the pattern are for the 5301 crystals.

• markings on the pattern are a random mix of seed beads and bugle beads.

Refer to Single Seed Bead technique on page 5, to sew on all the beads for this design.

For the first inch density connect all the beads.

For any beading involved beyond that distance, start and finish each bead separately.

After stitching on all the beads, the bag is ready to be sewn together. Refer to Stitching Instructions of Flat Base Handbags on page 50.

Make the beaded strap using the beaded strap instructions.

Bead configuration for beaded strap

1. 1 seed + 1 bugle bead + 1 seed.
2. 1 ceramic bead + 1 seed + 1 bugle bead + 1 x 5301 crystal + 1 seed + 1 bugle bead + 1 seed.
3. Repeat step 2, 14 times then repeat step 1 once.

Approximately finished strap length 43 cm (17 in).

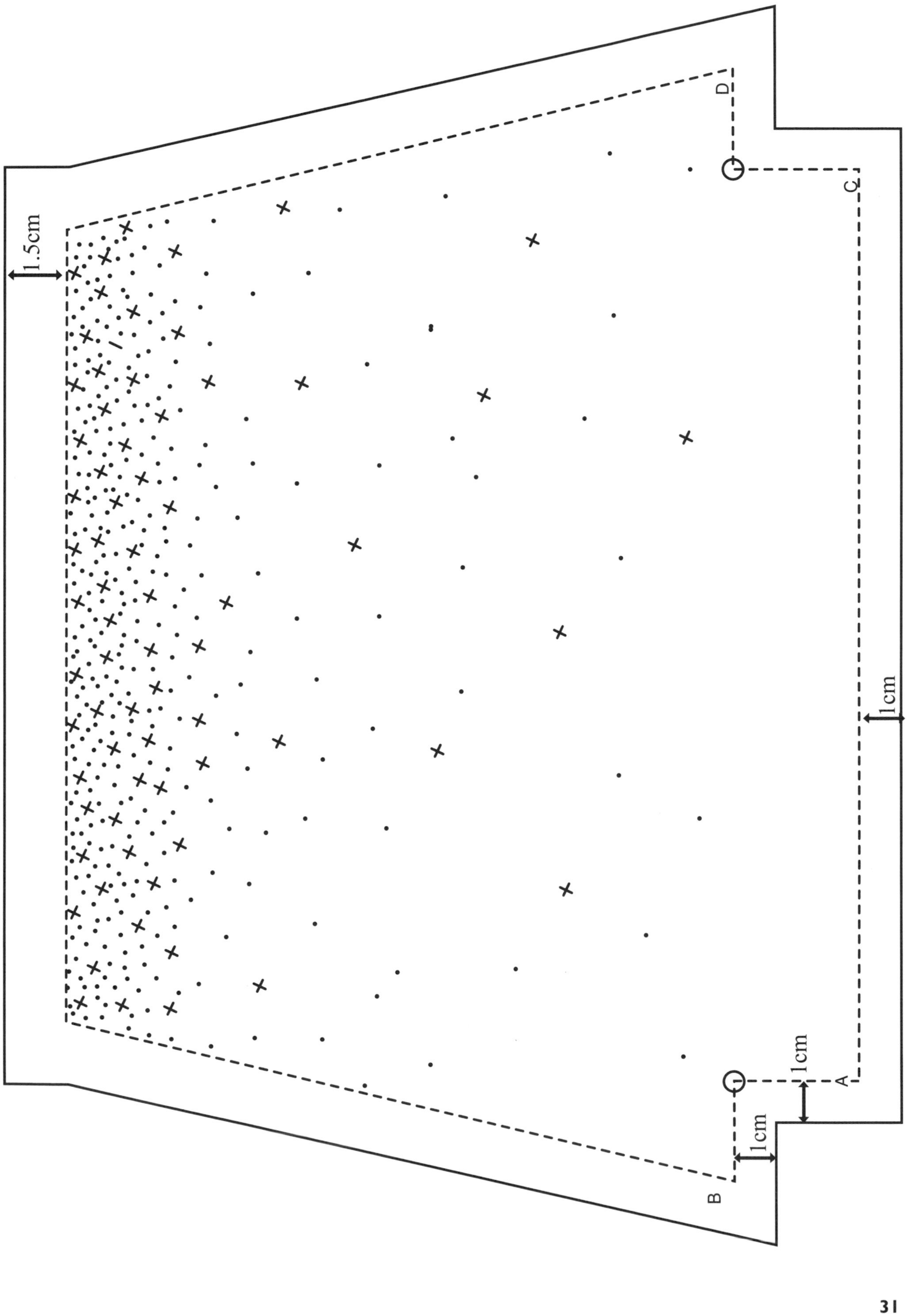

Gradation beaded handbag (80% of actual size)

1.5cm

1cm

1cm

1cm

1cm

A

B

C

D

Linear seed bead rose flower handbag

You will need

40 cm (16 in) silk duchess satin fabric
40 cm (16 in) woven fusible interfacing medium weight
40 cm (16 in) lining
1 spool 120 thick polycotton, colour to match beads
2 teaspoons 3 cut beads (green)
30 teaspoons seed beads, size 10 (black)
7 teaspoons seed beads, size 10 (red)
10 teaspoons seed beads, size 10 (silver-lined medium pink)
3 teaspoons seed beads, size 10 (light pink)
1 handle, shape of your choice, preferably metallic or plastic

Method

The effect of the beading in this handbag is to have all seed beads in lines.

Transfer the markings for the beading. Refer to Transferring a Design on page 2.

Begin with the outlines of all the flowers, buds and leaves in the centre of the bag. Refer to Straight Stitch Seed Beads technique on page 5.

Use these lines as a guide.

Work inwards from these outer lines, filling in any final gaps with the odd seed bead.

When the centre of the design is beaded, begin with the outer bag section.

The first row of beads should be a single row that outlines the flowers and leaves in the centre. This becomes the guideline.

All other lines of beading should follow this until you reach the outer straight sides of the bag.

Bring the seed beads up to the outer lines and no further.

When finished, give your work a gentle dry press face down underneath a towel. This will smooth out any uneven tension.

You are now ready to sew the bag together. Refer to Stitching Instructions for Rectangular Flat Bags on page 58.

1.5cm

1.5cm

Linear seed bead rose flower handbag (95% of actual size)

Flat seed encrusted stained glass handbag

You will need

40 cm (16 in) silk duchess fabric
40 cm (16 in) woven fusible interfacing medium weight
40 cm (16 in) lining
1 spool 120 thick polycotton, colour to match fabric
10 teaspoons of 3 cut seed beads (black)
10 teaspoons of 3 cut seed beads (blue iris)
6 teaspoons of 3 cut seed beads (red)
6 teaspoons of 3 cut seed beads (gold)
5 teaspoons of 3 cut seed beads (apricot)
1 handle, shape of your choice preferably metallic or plastic

Method

Transfer the markings for the beading. Refer to Transferring a Design on page 2.

Begin with beading the rectangular outline of the bag and all the lattice outlines. Refer to Straight Stitch Seed Bead technique on page 5.

Fill in the third centre row of the lattice work using the same method as above.

This bag can be beaded on a ring frame. See Beading on a Ring Frame technique on page 10.

If you choose this option you would now set up your work on the frame.

Bead all the shape spaces, filling in the whole area. Refer to Single Seed Bead technique on page 5. Try and bead the seed beads in all different directions, keeping the beads as close as possible.

Continue with the above step until all the spaces are filled.

Give your work a gentle dry press face down underneath a towel. This will smooth out any uneven tension.

You are now ready to sew the bag together. Refer to Stitching Instructions for Rectangular Flat Bags on page 58.

1.5cm

1.5cm

Flat seeeded encrusted stained glass handbag (95% of actual size)

3D encrusted art nouveau rose antique style handbag

You will need

40 cm (16 in) Thai silk fabric
40 cm (16 in) woven fusible interfacing medium weight
40 cm (16 in) lining fabric
1 spool 120 thick polycotton, colour to match fabric
30 cm (12 in) handbag chain
2 x 'O' rings to use as a handle
1 x size BL56 rectangular handbag clasp
5 teaspoons seed beads, size 11 (matte silver in photo)
6 teaspoons seed beads, size 10 (light blue seed in photo)
4 teaspoons 3 cut seed beads (cornflower blue in photo)
1 small to medium tassel, colour to match bag and beading
4 teaspoons seed beads, size 10 (light silver in photo)
3 teaspoons seed beads, size 10 (dark blue seed in photo)
2 teaspoons 2 cut seed beads (dark silver in photo)

Method

Transfer the markings for the beading. Refer to Transferring a Design on page 2.

Start by beading the outer spaced lines. Refer to Single Seed Bead technique on page 5.

Keep a space of 0.5 cm (¼ in) in between each bead.

Bead the outline of the rose. Refer to Single Seed Bead technique, but keep your spacing between each bead absolutely minimal.

Fill in the petals and leaves of the flower. Refer to Triple Seed Loop Encrusting technique on page 8.

When all petals are beaded you are ready to stitch your bag together. Refer to Stitching Instructions for Antique Handbags on page 54.

Attach the tassel to the lower point of the bag by hand stitching it to the point. Start and finish off stitching either invisibly or on the inside of the bag.

Bring your newly threaded needle to the top of the tassel. Thread on enough beads to reach the stitching on the tassel loop. Take your needle down invisibly through the loop to secure the end. Repeat this step 5 or 6 times at different parts of the tassel so some beading is incorporated into your tassel.

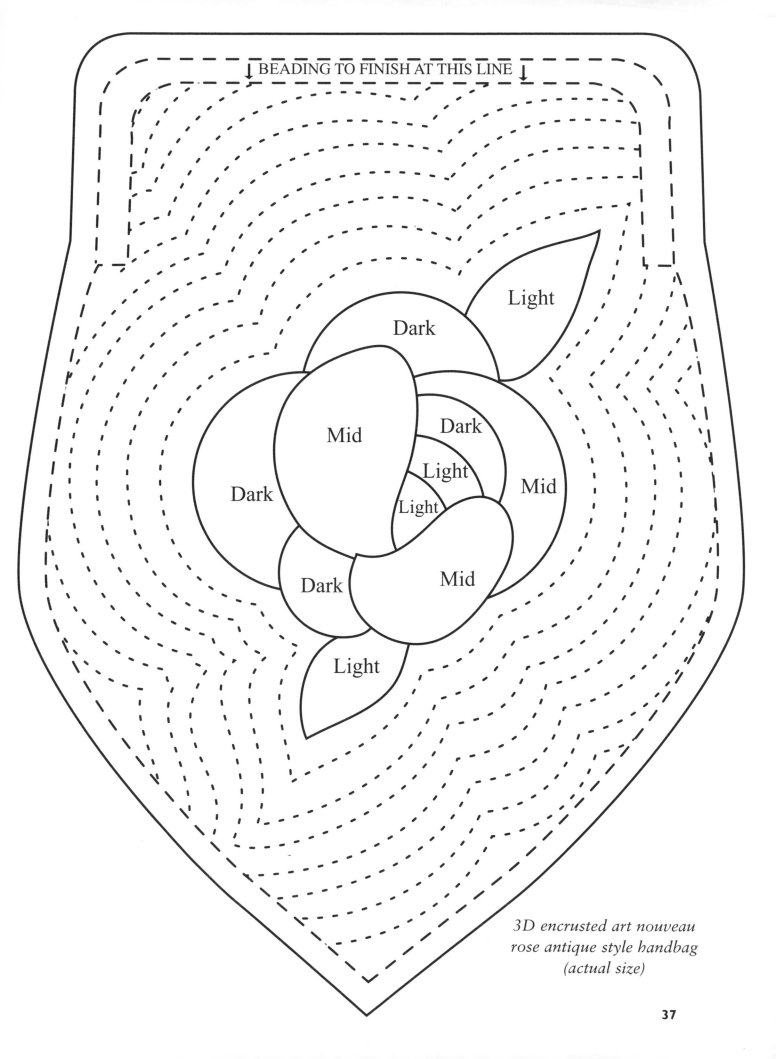

BEADING TO FINISH AT THIS LINE

Light

Dark

Mid

Dark

Dark

Light

Light

Mid

Dark

Mid

Light

3D encrusted art nouveau rose antique style handbag (actual size)

37

Swirl flower beaded antique style handbag

You will need

30 cm (11¾ in) delustered satin fabric
30 cm (11¾ in) woven fusible interfacing medium weight
30 cm (11¾ in) lining fabric
1 spool 120 thick polycotton, colour to match fabric
40 cm (16 in) tiger tail
2 crimps
5 teaspoons 2 cut beads (for lines and base roses, trim for clasp)
5 teaspoons bugle beads, size 2 (leaves)
½ teaspoon 6 mm flat sequins
6 pcs x small marquis crystals
18 pcs x 4 mm pressed crystals
3 teaspoons seed beads, size 10 (roses)
1 handbag clasp size BL56

Method

Transfer the markings for the beading. Refer to Transferring a Design on page 2.

Bead the outer lines/stems of the flowers. Refer to Straight Stitch Seed Beads technique on page 5.

Bead the outer lines of the leaves in the centre of the bag. Refer to BB Straight Stitch Bugle Beads technique on page 4. Fill in the leaves using the same method. Work from the outside of the leaves inwards. Try to brick the bugle beads as much as possible as this is a much neater and visually pleasing effect. See diagram on page 6.

Bead the outline of the top flowers and the circle at the base of the flowers. Refer to Straight Stitch Seed Beads technique.

Fill in each base circle with the 4 mm crystals and size 10 seed beads. Refer to Single Seed Bead technique on page 5, stitching the crystals on singularly first and then fill in the small spaces in between the crystals with the size 10 seed beads.

Stitch on the fanning bugle beads within the flowers. Start from the base circle and work outward with each stitch. Your beads will naturally want to fan in this direction. Refer to BB Straight Stitch Bugle Beads techniques, steps 1-7 for each bugle bead.

Stitch on the marquis crystals. Refer to Seed Bead Anchor (centre hole) technique on page 6. Use this method for each side hole. Use size 10 seed bead to anchor your crystal.

Fill in the top outline of the flower. Refer to Triple Seed Loop Encrusting technique on page 8. Thread on the following for this method: 1 x seed size 10 + 1 x 2 cut seed + 1 x seed size 10. Keep your beading close together.

Bead the sequins on. Refer to Seed Bead Anchor (centre hole) technique. Finish off after each cluster or singular sequin.

Give your work a gentle dry press face down underneath a towel. This will smooth out any uneven tension. Sew the bag together. Refer to Stitching Instructions for Antique Handbags on page 54.

Make the beaded strap a finished length of 34 cm (13⅜ in). Refer to Beaded Strap Instructions on page 59. Use 2 cut beads to form strap.

Swirl flower beaded antique style handbag (actual size)

Loose loop and fringed handbag

You will need

20 cm (8 in) delustered satin fabric
20 cm (8 in) woven fusible interfacing medium weight
20 cm (8 in) lining
140 grams 3 cut beads (approximately ¾ metric cup)

Method

Begin by stitching the bag together. Refer to Stitching Instructions for a Rectangle Flat bag on page 58. Using only Steps 4-10.

Leave the lining open at the bottom of the handbag.

Transfer the markings for the beading. Refer to Transferring a Design on page 2.

Stitch the beads down the 2 marked lines and on each side seam. Refer to Single Seed Bead technique on page 5. These form the anchor beads. Make sure to stitch them closely so there are no gaps. This is important when you come to bead the cross loops.

Make sure the hole of your bead crosses the marked line at a 90° angle. See diagram below.

You must stitch exactly the same number of beads on every line and side seam. Finish off after each line.

For the cross loops: bring the double threaded needle up through your fabric to the right side, right next to the bead at one of the side seams.

Take your needle through the anchor bead.

Thread approximately 30 x 3 cut beads onto your needle. This number of beads should fit easily into the space between the two anchor rows.

Thread your needle through the next anchor bead.

Repeat the above 2 steps until the beading line is complete, across the face of the bag.

Take your needle through the last bead on the line at the other side seam.

Thread on 1 x 3 cut bead onto your needle then thread your needle through the anchor bead below it to begin beading the next line, working in the opposite direction.

Repeat these steps until the beading on the whole handbag is finished. Start and finish off at either side seam.

Stitch the strap. Bead the strap as you did the handbag. The loops will run along the length of the strap rather than across the width.

Machine stitch the inner lining together at the bottom edge of the bag and hand stitch the strap to the handbag on the inside of the bag at the centre top edge.

top

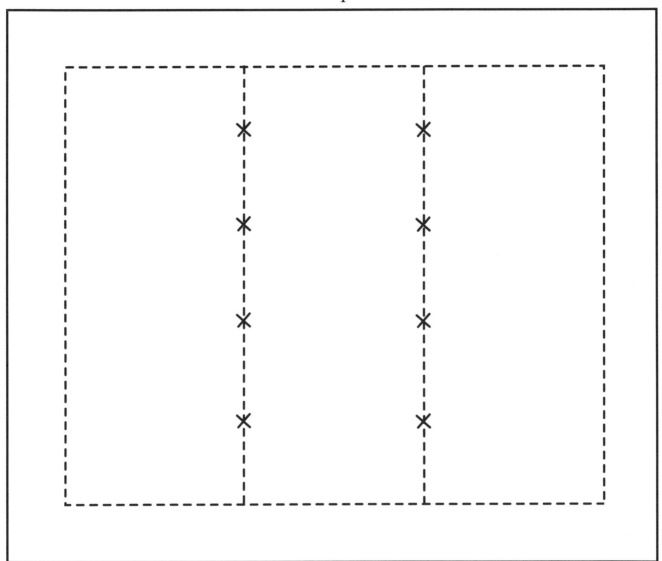

Loose loop and fringed handbag (actual size)

Leaf flower antique style handbag

You will need

40 cm (16 in) Thai silk fabric
40 cm (16 in) woven fusible interfacing medium weight
40 cm (16 in) lining fabric
1 spool 120 thick polycotton, colour to match beads
4 teaspoons of seed beads, size 10 (vines and leaves)
2 teaspoons of bugle beads, size 2 (flowers)
40 teaspoons of 3 cut beads (background)
2 teaspoons of bugle beads, size 3 (leaf centres)
6 pcs x 4 mm pressed crystals (flower centres)
1 handbag clasp size BL56

Method

Stitch the vines and leaves first. Refer to Straight Stitch Seed Bead technique on page 5.

Make sure you have a single seed bead at the point of your leaf. This will give it a nice elongated shape and a better finish.

Bead the centres of the leaves with 1 size 3 bugle bead per leaf. The bugle bead should fit neatly into the unbeaded central space.

Refer to BB Straight Stitch Bugle Beads technique steps 1–7 on page 4.

Next bead the flowers. Keep the marked hole in the centre, free of any beading. Start attaching each bugle bead from this central point and radiate the beads out with your stitch.

Stitch in the flower centre after you have stitched all your bugle bead petals. Refer to the Single Seed Bead technique on page 5. Finish off each flower separately.

This bag can be beaded on a ring frame. See Instructions for Beading on a Ring Frame on page 10.

If you choose this option, you would now set up your work on the frame.

Fill in the background. Refer to Single Seed Bead technique. Try to bead your seed beads in all different directions keeping the beads close together.

Only bead to 0.5 cm (¼ in) away from the handbag stitching line and fill in the rest of the beads when you have sewn the outer bag together.

Give your work a gentle dry press face down underneath a towel. This will smooth out any uneven tension.

You are now ready to sew the bag together. Refer to Stitching Instructions for Antique Handbags on page 54.

Once you have sewn your bag together, fill in the spaces around the outer edge of the bags with more 3 cut beads.

BEADING TO FINISH AT THIS LINE

Leaf flower antique style handbag (actual size)

Radiating antique style handbag

You will need

40 cm (16 in) delustered satin fabric
40 cm (16 in) woven fusible interfacing medium weight
40 cm (16 in) lining fabric
1 spool 120 thick polycotton, colour to match fabric
7 teaspoons of bugle beads, size 2 (dividing rays)
30 teaspoons of bugle beads, size 2 (fill in)
1 x 8 mm gold pearl
5 pcs x medium teardrop silver foiled crystal
2 teaspoons of seed beads, size 8 (gold for centre encrusting)
1 teaspoon seed beads, size 10 (white for centre encrusting)

Method

Transfer the markings for the beading. Refer to Transferring a Design on page 2.

Begin work on the bugle bead dividing rays.

Start at the edge of the central shape and stitch outwards towards the outer stitching line. Refer to BB Straight Stitch Bugle Beads technique on page 4.

Fill in the space between each dividing ray using the same stitch as above.

Work from the edge of the dividing rays inwards, trying to brick the bugle beads as much as possible. See diagram below and on page 6.

When all the radiating lines are complete, fill in the central shape, between the radiating lines.

Bead the centre point last.

Begin with the gold pearl in the centre. Refer to Single Seed Bead technique on page 5.

Stitch the 5 teardrop crystals in place evenly around the central pearl.

Encrust the space left with the seed beads. Refer to Triple Seed Loop Encrusting technique on page 8.

Thread the beads as follows: 1 x seed size 8 + 1 x seed size 10 + 1 x seed size 8.

When you have finished encrusting you are ready to sew the bag together.

Refer to Stitching Instructions for Antique Handbags on page 54.

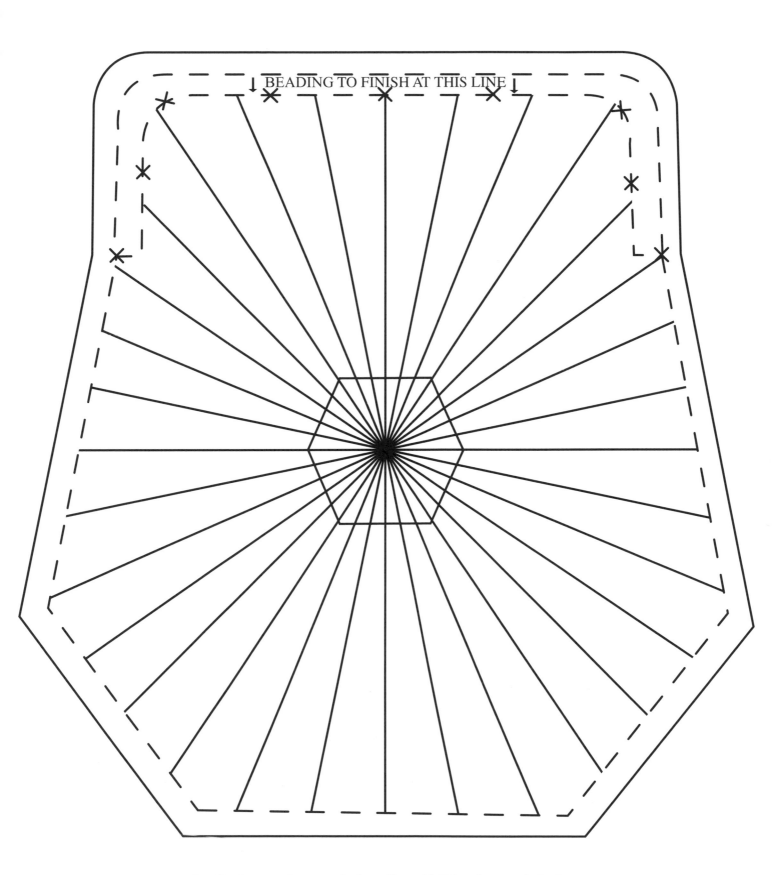

Radiating antique style handbag (95% of actual size)

Geometric antique style handbag

You will need

40 cm (16 in) delustered satin fabric
40 cm (16 in) woven fusible interfacing medium weight
40 cm (16 in) lining
1 spool 120 thick polycotton, colour to match beads
20 teaspoons bugle beads, size 2 (gold)
10 teaspoons bugle beads, size 2 (red)
10 teaspoons bugle beads, size 3 (light blue)
10 teaspoons bugle beads size 3 (aqua)
1 rectangular handbag clasp size BL56
30 cm (12 in) handbag chain

Method

Transfer the markings for the beading. Refer to Transferring a Design on page 2.

Start by beading all the outer lines of the geometric shapes.

Be sure to keep lines straight. Refer to BB Straight Stitch Bugle Bead technique on page 4.

At the points, overlap one bugle bead slightly across the top of the bugle bead it forms a join with. See diagram below.

This will create a neat point.

When you have beaded all the outer lines (the marked lines), fill in each section.

Start from the sections outer lines and work inwards. Be sure to brick your beads as often as possible for a nice neat effect. See bricking diagram below.

When you have finished filling all the sections, give your work a gentle dry press face down underneath a towel. This will smooth out any uneven tension.

You are now ready to sew the bag together. Refer to Stitching Instructions for an Antique Handbag on page 54.

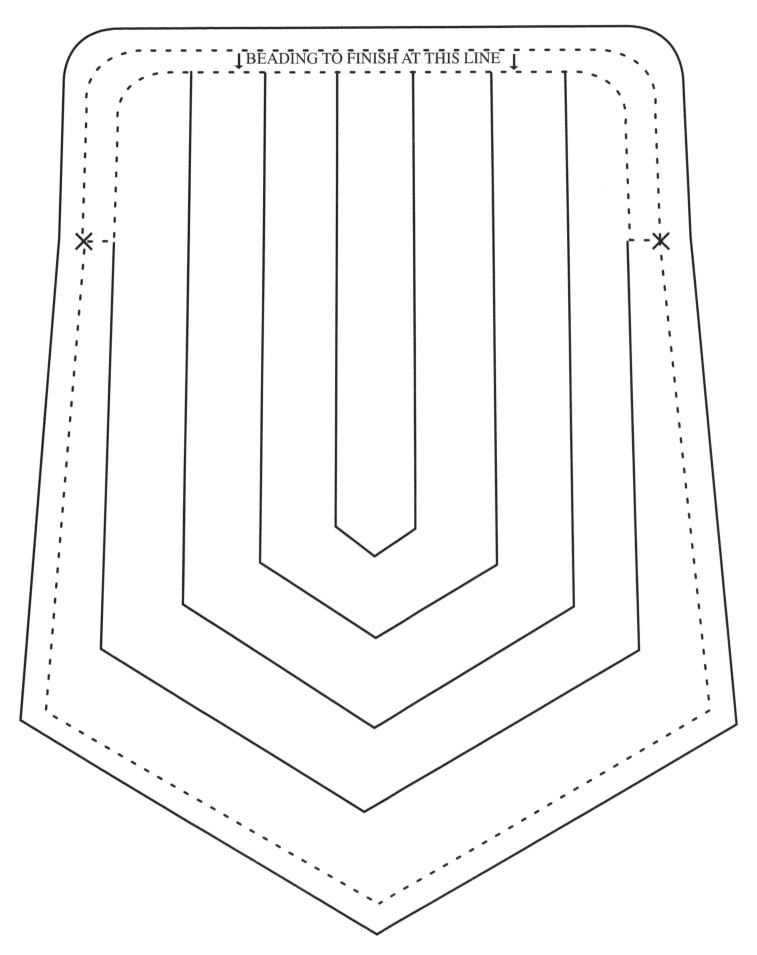

↓ BEADING TO FINISH AT THIS LINE ↓

Geometric antique style handbag (actual size)

Left: Chinese brocade shoulder bag with hanging beading
Right: Chinese brocade shoulder bag with bead loops

Left: Beaded loop handbag

Right: Linear seed bead rose flower handbag

Left: 3D encrusted art nouveau rose antique style handbag

Right: Flat sequin flower and seed spray handbag

Stitching
Instructions

Stitching instructions for flat base handbags

Step 1: Cut 2 pieces of lining and 2 pieces of fabric. Cut 2 strap pieces 4 cm (1½ in) x 33 cm (13 in) each strap. Cut 2 pieces of roping (cotton cord) 40.5 cm (16 in).

Step 2: Fold strap pieces in half lengthwise. Pin along the long edge and stitch along using 0.5 cm (¼ in) seam allowance.

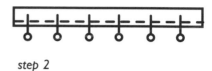

step 2

Step 3: Turn the straps through to the right side, thread the roping (cotton cording) through the strap. Leave an even amount of rope exposed at each end. The roping (cotton cording) should be pulled firm in the strap channel.

step 3

Step 4: Unravel the exposed end of each side of the roping (cotton cording) back to point where the roping enters the channel. Lay the roping flat and pin flat, pinning through all layers. Stitch 0.5 cm (¼ in) from the edge.

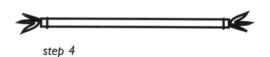

step 4

Step 5: Pin and tack the straps to the right sides of the fabric where the 'V' marks indicate the centre of the strap.

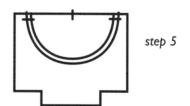

step 5

Step 6: Pin the lining to the fabric, right sides together, along the top long straight edge. Stitch using 1.5 cm (⅝ in) seam allowance.

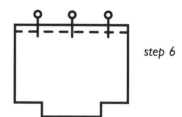

step 6

Step 7: Press with the seam turnings toward the lining. Pin stitch 1 mm away from the seam on the lining right side. Press a sharp fold at the seam where the lining and fabric are stitched together.

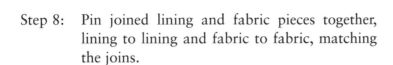

step 7

Step 8: Pin joined lining and fabric pieces together, lining to lining and fabric to fabric, matching the joins.

Step 9: Stitch across the base of the bag for both the fabric and lining. Use 1 cm (³/₈ in) seam allowance.

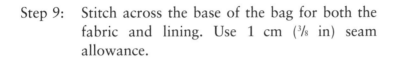

steps 8, 9, 10

Step 10: Stitch down the sides of the bag, these are the long edges. Use 1.5 cm (⁵/₈ in) seam allowance. Leave a 5 cm (2 in) opening in the side of the lining, so you can turn the bag through.

Step 11: Open out the side seams and base seam. Bring points C and D together, and A and B together and pin along this edge.

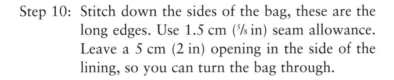

step 11

Step 12: Stitch along this edge using 1cm (³/₈ in) seam allowance. Trim the seam allowance back to half.

Step 13: Turn the bag through and press.

Step 14: Turn the raw edges of the side opening in and pin stitch this edge together.

Stitching instructions for shoulder bags

Step 1: Cut out the fabric and lining pieces, 2 pieces of each. Cut 2 straps, 60 cm (23¾ in) x 7 cm (2¾ in) each.

Step 2: Fold the strap in half lengthwise. Pin the edges together. Stitch along the long edge using 1 cm (³⁄₈ in) seam allowance. Turn through and press with the seam allowance on the side. Edge stitch both long edges of the strap.

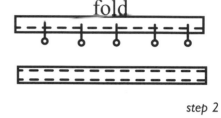

step 2

Step 3: Fold down the 8 cm (3⅛ in) of the fabric edge and press.

step 3

Step 4: Match the centre mark of the fabric with the centre mark of the lining. Repeat for the other side.

Step 5: Pin this edge right sides together and stitch using 1 cm (³⁄₈ in) seam allowance. Back tack at each end.

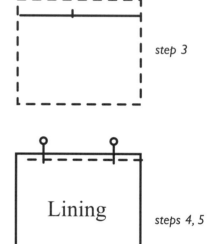

steps 4, 5

Step 6: Open the bag out and press all seam turnings towards the lining.

Step 7: Pin stitch 1 mm away from the seam on the right side of the lining. Repeat with the other pieces. Press a sharp fold at this seam on both pieces.

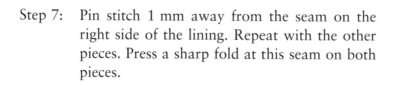

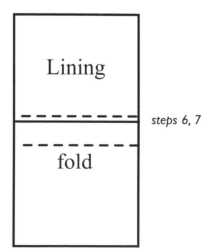

steps 6, 7

52

Step 8: Pin right sides together, lining with lining and fabric with fabric. Stitch along each long edge and the bottom of the fabric, using 1.5 cm (⅝ in) seam allowance

Step 9: Clip the corners. Turn through to the right side and press. Turn raw edges of bottom edge of lining in and pin stitch along this edge.

Step 10: Tuck lining into the bag. Hand stitch the press stud onto the inside of the bag near the centre top edge.

Step 11: Ditch stitch in the side seams, stitching the lining to the bag for a depth of 2.5 cm (1 in).

Step 12: Divide the bag top of the bag into 4 even sections and mark with chalk. Pin the straps to the 2nd and 3rd marks, 2.5 cm (1 in) down from the top edge marked with large dots. Pin into place with the edges of the straps pinned under.

Step 13: Machine stitch the straps down along their edges and stitch a rectangle at the end of each strap.

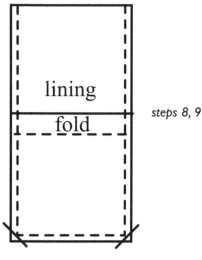

lining

fold

steps 8, 9

S.S

step 11

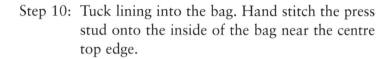

step 12

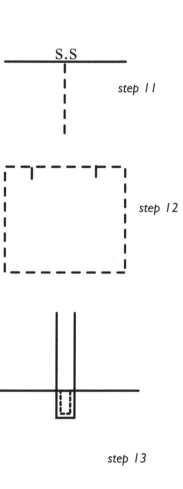

step 13

Stitching instructions for antique handbags

Step 1: Cut out the fabric and lining pieces, cut 2 pieces of each.

Step 2: Pin 1 lining piece to 1 fabric piece, right sides together at the top edge of the bag. Stitch from x to x using 0.5 cm (¼ in) seam allowance. Clip into the x mark, being careful not to clip into the stitching. Repeat for the other side.

Step 3: Turn the top of the bag through to the right side. Press the seam edge.

Step 4: Pin the right sides of the fabric pieces together along the side seams and bottom edge.

Step 5: Stitch along the fabric side seams and the bottom of the bag using 0.5 cm (¼ in) seam allowance.

Step 6: Fold the fabric part of the bag inwards and out of the way of the lining.

Step 7: Pin the lining side seams together with right sides facing. Stitch using 0.5 cm (¼ in) seam allowance. Leave the bottom of the bag lining open so you can turn your bag through to the right side.

Step 8: Turn the bag through. Press. Turn the raw edges of the bottom edge of the lining in and pin stitch this edge together.

Step 9: Take your bag and clasp. Find the centre of your bags front and back. Match these points up with the centre of the clasp and the side seams with the sides of the clasp.

Step 10: Wedge the beaded edge up against the edge of the clasp. Push the fabric turnings in behind the lip on the back of the clasp.

Step 11: Hold the turnings in place whilst you hand stitch the bag to the clasp. Stitch one side at a time. Work slip stitches to secure it.

Step 12: Stitch on a beaded trim if you require your stitches to be hidden. Simply thread on 2-3 seed beads in between each hole on the clasp, when you bring your needle up to the right side of the fabric. They will be secured in place when you take your needle through the clasp to the wrong side of the fabric.

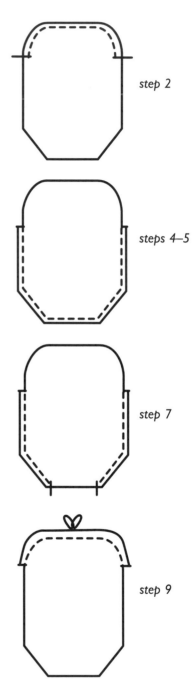

step 2

steps 4–5

step 7

step 9

Stitching instructions for single loop handbags

Step 1: Cut 2 pieces of lining and 2 pieces of fabric. Cut 1 strap 24 cm (9½ in) x 4 cm (1½ in) in fabric and from interfacing. Bond the interfacing to the wrong side of the fabric.

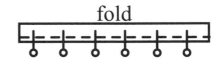

fold

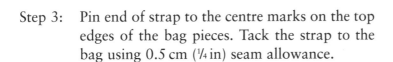

step 2

Step 2: Fold strap in half lengthwise. Pin the edges together. Stitch along the long edge using 0.5 cm (¼ in) seam allowance. Turn through and press with seam on one side of the strap.

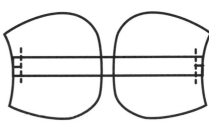

step 3

Step 3: Pin end of strap to the centre marks on the top edges of the bag pieces. Tack the strap to the bag using 0.5 cm (¼ in) seam allowance.

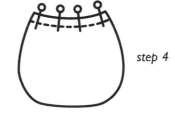

step 4

Step 4: Pin 1 lining piece to 1 fabric piece right sides together. Stitch along the top edge using 0.5 cm (¼ in) seams. Repeat for other side of the bag. Stitch one side of the bag at a time to avoid catching in the straps in the wrong places.

step 5

Step 5: Clip into the seam allowance around the stitched edge.

Step 6: Press all turnings toward lining. Pin stitch 1 mm away from the seam on the right side of the lining. Press a sharp fold at the seam where the lining and fabric are stitched together.

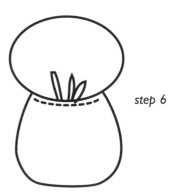

step 6

Step 7: Pin the bag pieces together. Fabric pieces right sides together and lining pieces right sides together. Make sure that the strap is not twisted the wrong way.

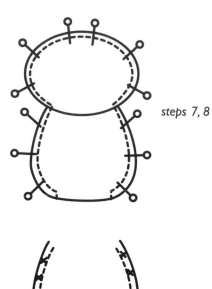

steps 7, 8

Step 8: Leave an opening approximately 5 cm (2 in) in the stitching at the bottom of the lining. Stitch around the outer edge using 1 cm (³/₈ in) seam allowance.

Step 9: Trim the seam allowance back to 0.5 cm (¼ in). Clip small 'V's out of the outer edge, to make the curve more defined. Turn the bag through to the right side. Press.

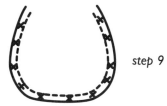

step 9

Step 10: Turn the raw edges of the bottom opening in and pin stitch this edge together.

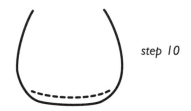

step 10

Stitching instructions for top edge of flat base handbags

Step 1: Cut out the double bonded fabric and lining, cut 2 pieces of lining and 2 pieces of fabric.

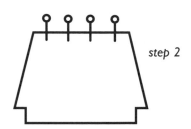

step 2

Step 2: Pin, together along the top edge, 1 piece of lining and 1 piece of fabric, with right sides together. Repeat to form other piece.

Step 3: Stitch along this edge using 1 cm seam allowance. Back tack at each end.

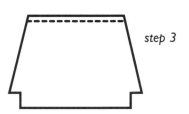

step 3

Step 4: Open the bag out and press all seam turnings towards the lining.

Step 5: Pin stitch 1mm away from the seam on the right side of the lining.

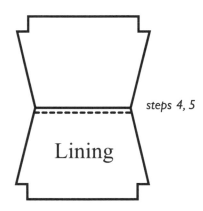

steps 4, 5

Lining

Step 6: Press a sharp fold at the seam where the lining and fabric are stitched together. Naturally the lining will roll in slightly more. This makes the seam more invisible.

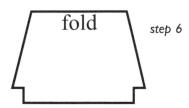

fold

step 6

Stitching instructions for rectangular flat bags

Step 1: Cut out the fabric and lining pieces, 2 pieces of each. Cut 2 pieces 8 cm (3 ¼ in) x 10 cm (4 in) each.

Step 2: Pin small pieces together, right sides facing, along the 10 cm (4 in) edges. Stitch using 1 cm (³/₈ in) seam allowance.

Step 3: Turn through and press. Bring both raw edges together. Align the centre of the raw edges on this piece to the centre of the right side of the bag edge. Use 1 cm (³/₈ in) seam allowance.

Step 4: Pin bag pieces together at the top edge, 1 piece of lining to 1 piece of fabric, with right sides together. Repeat for the other piece.

Step 5: Stitch edge together using 1.5 cm (³/₈ in) seam allowance. Back tack at each end.

Step 6: Open the bag out and press all seam turnings towards the lining.

Step 7: Pin stitch 1 mm away from the seam on the right side of the lining. Repeat with the other pieces. Press a sharp fold at this seam on both pieces.

Step 8: Pin right sides together, lining facing lining and fabric facing fabric. Stitch along each long edge and the bottom of the fabric using 1.5 cm (⁵/₈ in) seam allowance.

Step 9: Clip the fabric corners. Turn through and press. Turn raw edges of bottom edge of the lining in and pin stitch this edge together.

Step 10: Tuck lining into the bag. Hand stitch the press stud onto the inside of the case near the top edge in the centre. Attach handle through fabric loop at top of bag.

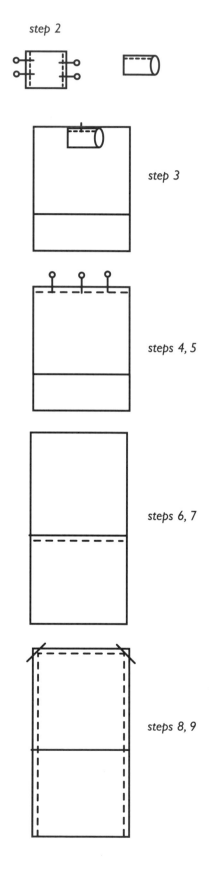

step 2

step 3

steps 4, 5

steps 6, 7

steps 8, 9

Beaded strap instructions

Small nosed pliers are necessary for this step.

Thread 1 crimp (small silver metal bead) onto the tiger tail.

Thread the tiger tail through again to form a small loop.

Take pliers and close crimp onto the tiger tail. Use force!

Thread on your beads until the beaded length equals the length specified in the individual bag instructions.

Thread on another crimp and make another loop as you did at first.

It makes it easier if you thread the free end of the tiger tail back through a few beads.

Clamp down hard on the crimp.

You should now have a firm beaded strap.

Trim off any excess tiger tail.

Hand stitch these loops to the sides or side seams of your bag, as specified, preferably on the inside of your bag.

Index